Journey
to the top
of the World

BY JANET FOSTER

Prentice Hall Books for Young Readers
A Division of Simon & Schuster Inc.
New York

Text © 1987 Janet Foster

Photographs used with permission:
p. 35 (John Torrington) Dr. Owen Beattie, University of Alberta;
pp. 48 & 49 (undersea dive) John Englander;
p. 49 (amphipods) William E. Cross, LGL Limited;
p. 72 (ancient sequoia site) Dr. Jane Francis.

All other photographs © 1987 John and Janet Foster

Design Director: Wycliffe Smith
Map: James Loates
Illustrations: Tony Delitala

Published by Prentice Hall Books for Young Readers
A Division of Simon & Schuster Inc.
Simon & Schuster Building Rockefeller Center
1230 Avenue of the Americas New York NY 10020

Originally published in Canada by Greey de Pencier Books, Toronto.

Prentice Hall Books for Young Readers is a trademark of
Simon & Schuster Inc.

Library of Congress Cataloging-in-Publication Data

Foster, Janet, 1940–
      Journey to the top of the world.

      Summary: Text and photographs present the plant and animal life
encountered on a journey across the Canadian Arctic and introduce
some of the permanent inhabitants and scientists who work there.
      1. Natural history—Canada, Northern—Juvenile literature.
2. Canada, Northern—Description and travel—Juvenile literature.
3. Natural history—Arctic regions—Juvenile literature. 4. Arctic
regions—Description and travel—Juvenile literature. [1. Natural
history—Canada, Northern. 2. Natural history—Arctic regions.
3. Canada, Northern. 4. Arctic regions] I. Title.

QH106.2.N55F67   1987   574.9719'9   87-18839
ISBN 0-13-511445-4

10 9 8 7 6 5 4 3 2 1

Contents

The Assignment

There is hardly a patch of free space left anywhere in our living room. The carpet is covered with bulky backpacks, small camp stoves, boxes of film, tripods and aluminum camera cases. In the big armchair, packages of freeze-dried food are stacked so high they are threatening to topple. And the sofa is half buried under tent, tarpaulins and sleeping bags. My husband, John, sits cross legged on the floor, nearly lost in the sea of equipment, ticking off items in the huge armloads of clothing I add to the steadily growing piles around him: jeans, shirts, extra sweaters, wool socks, boots, running shoes, parkas, raincoats, mittens, mosquito nets.... The list seems endless. But then it is not every day that we are sent on assignment to the Arctic. And what a plum assignment it is – a journey to the top of the world, photographing all the wild nature and wild creatures we'll see along the way. Our expedition will begin in spring on Canada's east coast and then, taking most of the summer, we'll travel up Labrador, across Baffin Island and into the High Arctic. Our final destination will be the most northern edge of our continent, the outer rim of North America. All winter long we have been planning the various stages of our journey: poring over maps, plotting the expeditions, pinpointing camping locations and preparing ourselves for a summer of high adventure. Now the months of planning and talking are over. It is March, and time to pack up and get ourselves ready for the first stage of our expedition. Filled with anticipation, my mind leaps ahead. By the middle of August, if all goes well, we will be camped at the top of the world.

The Route

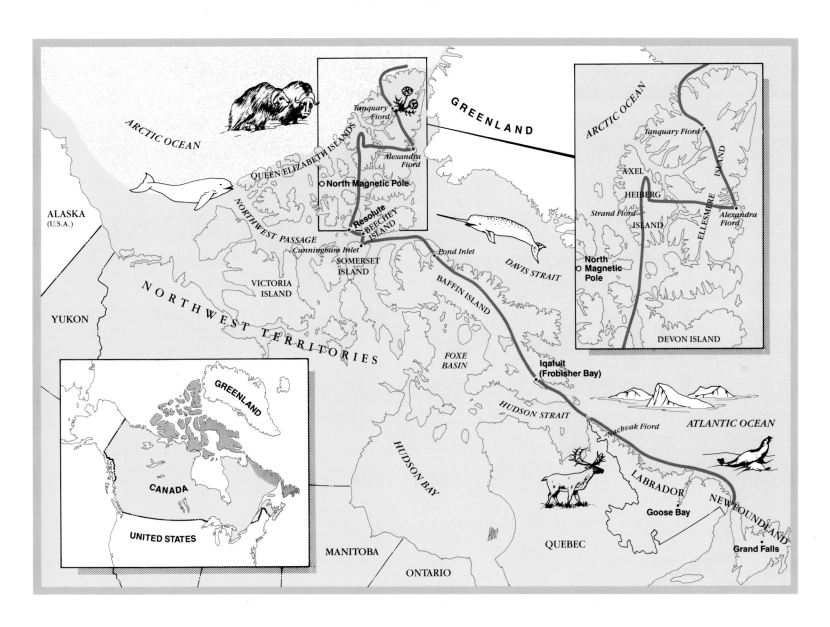

ARCTIC OCEAN

GREENLAND

Tanquary Fiord

Alexandra Fiord

North Magnetic Pole

QUEEN ELIZABETH ISLANDS

ALASKA (U.S.A.)

NORTHWEST PASSAGE

Resolute

BEECHEY ISLAND

Cunningham Inlet

SOMERSET ISLAND

Pond Inlet

DAVIS STRAIT

VICTORIA ISLAND

BAFFIN ISLAND

YUKON

N O R T H W E S T   T E R R I T O R I E S

FOXE BASIN

Iqaluit (Frobisher Bay)

HUDSON STRAIT

Nachvak Fiord

ATLANTIC OCEAN

HUDSON BAY

LABRADOR

NEWFOUNDLAND

MANITOBA

Goose Bay

ONTARIO

QUEBEC

Grand Falls

GREENLAND

CANADA

UNITED STATES

ARCTIC OCEAN

Tanquary Fiord

AXEL

HEIBERG

Strand Fiord

ISLAND

ELLESMERE ISLAND

Alexandra Fiord

North Magnetic Pole

DEVON ISLAND

5

Our Journey Begins

High above the glittering ice floes that blanketed the sea, our helicopter's whirling rotor blades sliced through the cold March air. Inside the chopper, John and I sat bundled up in our winter parkas, our faces pressed to the windows, nearly blinded by the dazzling brightness below. Eagerly we scanned each pan of ice, each broken floe. Where were the harp seals?

Back and forth we zoomed, searching first in one direction, then in another, as we headed farther and farther out to sea. Soon the fishing village we had left that morning became a small speck, and the coast of Newfoundland just a thin dark line behind us. On and on we flew, our pilot taking us in ever widening search patterns. I tried to use my binoculars to spot the seals ahead but there was so much vibration inside the chopper, I couldn't hold the glasses steady.

And then suddenly, we saw them. Small, dark, oblong shapes lying beside leads of open water that ran like avenues between the ice floes. The herd was large. From the air, there seemed to be hundreds of seals, scattered all over the ice. Our pilot flew high, trying not to disturb them while he searched for a safe landing spot. Then down we came, the big machine clattering noisily out of the sky. As the chopper's rubber pontoons gently touched and settled on the ice, most of the seals around us quickly disappeared into the sea, frightened by the arrival of such a strange mechanical creature.

Impatiently, we waited inside for the huge rotor blades to stop spinning and wind down. It seemed to take forever. With each passing second I grew more impatient. Finally the pilot gave us the thumbs-up signal. It was safe to get out. Gathering up our mittens and cameras, we thrust open the doors and stepped down onto the ice floe.

What a different world it was. How cold... and how blindingly bright. We landed on a level part of the floe, but all around us were tumbled ridges and huge blocks of gleaming blue ice. We stepped carefully around the open blow holes where the adult seals came up to breathe.

There was not a breath of wind, and as I moved away from the helicopter, I began to hear the sound of small voices, crying. There, lying on the smooth glittering floe or nestled down between the great chunks of ice, were the seal pups. At first we saw only their eyes. They were big, black and round, the blackest and roundest eyes I had ever seen. And in each one was a tiny teardrop. The pups' fur was thick and glossy and some of the coats were so creamy white, it was hard to see them against the brilliance of the ice.

Some of the pups were only a few days old and wailing loudly for their mothers. Soon the adult seals began to return, one by one. With one smooth, fluid movement they propelled their great sleek bodies up out of the water and back onto the ice. So long as John and I moved slowly and talked quietly, they did not seem to mind our being in their nursery. But one mother reared up aggressively and snorted when I came too close. Quickly, I positioned my tripod and then hesitated, nervously wondering what she would do. But after I had taken the first picture, she suddenly turned away and flopped back into the water, leaving me alone on the ice with her pup. Perhaps she had decided I was no threat to it. As I knelt down, two dark, luminous eyes gazed up at me inquisitively and a little wet nose with long whiskers burrowed into my mittened hand.

What wonderful creatures the pups were – so trusting, and so curious. They would slither over and try to push their black button noses right up against the camera lens each time we tried to take their pictures. Their coats were silky soft, and after I had finished filming one pup, it lolled back in my arms, head against my shoulder and eyes half closed. I thought it was the picture of happy contentment but a biologist later told us that the pup might have been in a trance. If suddenly faced with immediate danger, young seals can become so frightened that they slip into a kind of self-hypnotic state, not moving at all and scarcely breathing. Adult seals will sometimes go into similar trances.

It was amazing how each mother could find her own pup among all the others in the herd. Not only can she recognize its tiny calls, but she also knows her own pup by its very special smell, imprinted on her memory from the moment it is born. Each time she comes back up onto the ice, she has only to touch noses with the nearest pup, and sniff it. If it is her pup, recognition comes instantly. And she will accept no other. We saw many lonely youngsters left crying on the ice after being roughly rejected by the wrong mother. They would just have to wait for their own to return. One young pup, perhaps tired of waiting, slithered over and snuggled up beside one of the helicopter's black rubber pontoons. The bright sunlight had warmed the rubber and to the pup, the big pontoon must have seemed a lot like mother.

The pups were plump and full of milk. They nurse constantly during these first few weeks, and seal milk is rich in butterfat. By the time they are three weeks old, they will have tripled their birth weight, building up a thick layer of blubber under their fur to help protect them against the cold of the northern seas. In the coming months they would need all of that protection.

We shared the icy world of the seals for just a few hours. All too soon, our pilot called out and beckoned. It was time to go. The ice floe was shifting, and already larger cracks were beginning to appear.

As the chopper rose and clattered back toward the mainland we could see wider and wider leads opening in the ice. Soon the floes would crack and break apart. The ice would begin to melt and the adult seals would return to the sea and swim north. For a few weeks the pups would be abandoned, but then they, too, would begin a long migratory journey northward, swimming up the coast of Labrador to the waters of the High Arctic.

And what a wild and rugged coastline the pups swim by each summer. The bare rock mountains of Labrador are billions of years old and the land has been scraped, scoured and worn smooth by glaciers. This is the eastern edge of the Canadian Shield, made up of the oldest rocks in the world. Jacques Cartier, the explorer who voyaged to this forbidding part of North America in 1534, described it as "the land God gave to Cain," as a punishment. And a bare, harsh land it is, yet starkly beautiful.

Now it was early summer and we were continuing our arctic journey, flying up the coast in a small floatplane past towering headland cliffs and over wide bays that sparkled in the sunlight. Below us, drifting on the sea like mountains of polished porcelain, were icebergs. We circled over one that was so smooth and white it looked as though a passing giant had dropped a dollop of ice cream. The icebergs – hundreds of them – break off from the faraway glaciers of Greenland and come drifting south, carried on the cold Labrador Current. So many float down each year that sailors have called this treacherous stretch of coastline "Iceberg Alley."

Many of the icebergs drift into shallow bays and become grounded. The sun melts the ice, pieces break off, and, as the iceberg becomes lighter, it will float free, to drift on again. Some of these monsters can be at sea for a year, others as long as 10. One way to tell how long an iceberg has been drifting is to look for the old waterline marks, horizontal lines worn into the iceberg showing where once, perhaps months or even years earlier, it sat much lower in the sea.

11

Eager to see the icebergs close up, we landed in a sheltered bay. Water streamed out in great spumes behind the plane's metal floats as our pilot skimmed over the surface for a smooth landing. There was a large fishing boat anchored in the bay and after the day's catch of netted cod was secured in the hold, the captain kindly offered to take us out to see a few of the icebergs.

The icy giants towered above us, dwarfing the big fishing boat. Up close, they were awesome. And we were seeing only a small part of them. As much as nine-tenths of an iceberg's great mass lies hidden underwater. From the moment an iceberg breaks off a glacier and begins to drift, the sun, wind and wave action go to work, molding and sculpting it into fascinating shapes, patterns and textures. Some of the icebergs rose out of the sea in tall columns as smooth as glass; others were like mountains with lofty peaks and deep crevasses, and one had a perfectly round hole carved right through its centre. Fresh melt water streamed down their sides in sparkling rivulets and waterfalls, and from under the water the ice reflected the shades of the sea and glowed blue-green.

The captain was willing to take us close, but not too close. Icebergs can be very dangerous. All too frequently, huge chunks can break off without warning and the iceberg will suddenly pitch and roll over. I scooped up a small cube of ice from the sea and dropped it into my mug of water. As I swished it around, I heard strange fizzing, hissing, gurgling sounds as the air in the ice cube escaped.

That air was thousands of years old, trapped inside the ice when the glacier had formed. It was like listening to the last ice age.

Back on board the aircraft, we headed up the coast toward the northern tip of Labrador, flying over mountains whose snow-covered, craggy peaks were lost in low-hanging, misty clouds. What names they have! These are the Torngat Mountains and there, looming ahead of us, were the jagged, saw-toothed edges of Mount Razorback, its sheer rock walls guarding the entrance to Nachvak Fiord, our next destination. The plane banked sharply as the pilot turned and followed the long finger of salt water far inland to the head of the fiord. ''That's where you'll be camping,'' he called out to us as he pointed ahead.

But getting to our campsite was not easy. The shallow water was full of rocks and the pilot couldn't land us close. Instead, we waded ashore, carrying our heavy packs.

How hot it was! And so many blackflies! We pitched our tent, weighting the pegs and ropes down with big boulders. Some adventurous young mountain climbers were camped nearby and they warned us that winds could come streaming down the hillsides with such force they would blow our camp away. Legends say that the storm god, Torngarsoak, controls the mountain weather. As I batted the bothersome bugs that hung around my head in clouds, I wished out loud that he would send a few gentle winds our way. But none came. Perhaps Torngarsoak wasn't listening.

We cooked supper over an open fire on the beach, frying a fresh codfish the sea captain had given us, and topping the meal off with blueberries we had collected on shore. It had been a long day, full of adventure, and we had come a long way. I was tired and it felt good to slip into the sleeping bag. Later that night, in darkness, I heard the whoosh of a small whale surfacing in the bay. Sleepily, I wondered how it had found its way so far inland, a long way from the open sea.

Next morning we explored our surroundings, and soon discovered we were not the only ones being bothered and harassed by hordes of blackflies and mosquitoes. A small herd of caribou was down on a beach not far from our campsite, and being driven almost mad by the hungry insects. The caribou tore up and down the beach like racehorses, trying to escape, then splashed out into the cold water of the fiord to stand, quivering, in the deep water. There they would shake themselves, head to tail, like great dogs. We crept up cautiously but the tormented caribou seemed hardly aware of us – except for one huge bull with the biggest rack of antlers I had ever seen. It came charging down the beach toward me. Crouched behind my tripod, I felt my heart jump into my mouth. But at the last minute, the bull saw me. It came skidding to a stop, feet flying and wide hooves digging into the sand. Then it wheeled around and tore off in the opposite direction, the blackflies in hot pursuit. It all happened so fast, I wondered if the caribou had realized what I was.

There are three different species of caribou in the North: the barren-ground herds that roam restlessly through the Yukon and northwestern Canada; the small Peary caribou, found only among the islands of the High Arctic; and woodland caribou, here in northern Labrador. And it seemed to us they must be the biggest. Certainly they had the largest antlers, with huge shovels and points so gracefully shaped they looked like giant hands and fingers.

We hiked along the shore and came to a low area in the tundra where the grasses were tall, thick and very green. It was a startling contrast to the gray lichens and brown mosses of the surrounding tundra. We were puzzled at first, but then I caught a glimpse of gleaming whale bone. It was the remains of an ancient Eskimo house. Archaeologists look for these patches of lush green, for they are the telltale signs of early human habitation. They show up clearly, particularly from a low-flying aircraft. This house might have been 400 years old and the thick grasses grew where decaying refuse from centuries past had provided rich nutrients for the thin soil. Partly dug into the ground, the house would have had a roof made from whale bones covered by caribou skins and a floor of flat rock slabs. All that remained were a few ancient chunks of whale bone. One of them still formed part of the narrow entrance to a long tunnel leading inside.

High on the steep slope above the house site we discovered strange mounds of rock. Peering among the boulders, I saw white bones gleaming

in the dim light – human bones. These rock piles were the simple graves of people who had lived and died in Nachvak Fiord. With a sense of sadness, I realized that some of the graves belonged to children.

Scrambling back down the slope, I thought how tough and resourceful those people must have been to have lived in this harsh land. They would have sought shelter in winter around the inner islands or deep fiords, and then traveled out to the coast in spring to hunt harp seals on the ice. In summer, they moved to the outer islands to catch fish and waterfowl. And many times they would have made long, dangerous sea voyages up and down the coast, trading with other hunters and plying the treacherous waters in sturdy kayaks made from seal skins. Life for the ancestors of today's Eskimos (or Inuit, as they prefer to be called) could not have been easy. The sea gave them plenty of food, but each changing season brought them new tests of survival.

For three days we camped at Nachvak, hiking through the deep, U-shaped valleys that had been carved by retreating glaciers, and scrambling up steep slopes to the base of the sheer-walled granite mountains.

The climbers told us about a mountain called the Selamiut Tower. "Selamiut" means "sky dwellers," a word the early Eskimos used to describe the northern lights. To them, the strange patterns of blue and green moving across the night sky were the dancing spirits of the dead.

I could quite happily have spent another month exploring the wilderness of northern Labrador, but we were still a long way from our final destination. The Twin Otter was arriving next morning and it was time to move on again.

Whales Beneath the Ice

John spotted them first. "There they are," he yelled, pointing. "Two of them. There, where the sun is hitting the water!" I swung around and trained my binoculars on the spot. But it was too late. The whales had dived. All that remained on the dark surface was a swirl of sparkling water. Then, moments later and from right below us, we heard a great "whoosh," the sound of whales expelling air as they came to the surface to refill their lungs. A pod of six was cruising by under our cliff-top perch, and so close we did not need binoculars to identify them. Narwhals!

Smoothly and effortlessly, the whales glided through the water beneath us. Some were a silvery blue-gray, others mottled with lighter shadings of brown and white. These were all male narwhals, and as they swam by us their spiraled ivory tusks shone through the still black water like long white swords. They moved at the same speed, and in tight formation: three ahead, three behind. Then, as if on a silent signal, they arched their backs, rolled forward and dived in unison, leaving behind patterns of ever-widening ripples.

We watched and waited...keeping our eyes fixed on the ripples and hoping the narwhals would reappear. Long minutes passed. The sea became very still once more. But when they finally surfaced again, the whales were far away and moving on steadily up the coast.

The midnight sun shone brightly, and as we picked our way among the huge rocks and boulders on the hillside above the inlet, we heard other narwhals come up between the ice floes to blow and breathe. Their exhaled breath hung in the cold air, forming vapor clouds to mark the spot where they had surfaced. Backlit by the low sun, the small clouds looked like misty, golden balloons. To have had such a good look at a pod of narwhals on our first night in Pond Inlet seemed a good omen. Walking back to the small lodge where we were staying in the village, our heads were full of questions. How many narwhals were there? Where were they going? Where had they come from? And more importantly, how could we get close enough to photograph them?

It was the mysterious narwhals that had brought us to Pond Inlet, an Inuit village perched on Baffin Island's northern coast. We had arrived earlier that day, flying in on the regular passenger service that links the small northern communities throughout the Arctic. The route took us over the long mountain range whose snowy peaks and glacier-filled valleys form the spine of Baffin, the largest island in Canada. We flew over the mountain featured in the opening scene of a James Bond movie – a daredevil stuntman skis right off the mountaintop's flat plateau, hurtles out into space, and then opens a parachute!

Close to 900 people live in the village of Pond Inlet. At the turn of the century it was still a whaling station and many Inuit families lived in camps along the coastline. But as the station grew, slowly turning into a village and providing goods and services, and government housing, the Inuit moved in from the outlying camps and took up permanent residence.

Today in Pond Inlet there is a school, a post office, a nursing station and dental clinic, a Royal Canadian Mounted Police detachment and a Hudson's Bay Company store where you can buy everything from groceries to seal skins. The younger children stay in Pond for their primary and elementary schooling, but after Grade 10 they must move to Iqaluit (Frobisher Bay), or even farther south, to complete their education. This means separation from family and friends for months at a time. And having to go away is never easy.

Walking back from our whale-watching that first night, I thought Pond Inlet must be one of the prettiest communities in the Arctic. The small frame houses, nestled into the rocks along the shore, were bathed in a soft, golden light. Out in the bay, broken ice floes nudged and jostled each other gently as the tide flowed out, and on the far side of the inlet rose the mountainous snow-capped peaks of Bylot Island. Wreathed in haloes of wispy pink clouds, they, too, were tinged gold by the midnight sun.

In summer, it's hard to think of "day" and "night" in the Arctic. It's even harder to tell the difference between morning and afternoon. All day – and all night – the sun travels endlessly around the sky in a big circle. Even when your watch tells you it is bedtime, you really don't feel tired. At three o'clock in the morning, when I was trying to block out the sunlight by taping the curtains to the window, I could still hear village children laughing and playing in the street.

Next morning was the start of a holiday weekend in Pond Inlet, the first long weekend of the summer, and many families were down on the beach loading the open boats. Most were going out to summer camps along the coast for a weekend of hunting and fishing. Boxes of food, packs, fishing rods, rifles, and caribou skins for sleeping on were being piled into the boats. Even the big-wheeled motorized tricycles were hauled aboard.

Although the Inuit now live and work in Pond Inlet, they still love the land, and going out to camp is part of their tradition and culture. The children seemed most excited of all, scampering about the beach or standing impatiently while their mothers pulled extra-warm sweaters and light parkas over their heads. It would be cold among the ice floes.

Soon everyone was off and away, the small flotilla of boats picking its way slowly and carefully through the ice, searching for the open leads. The happy voices and drone of outboard motors faded away in the distance. Now we wondered how we would spend the long weekend. With so many of the townsfolk gone, the village was going to be very quiet. We had no boat, and the aircraft was not coming to pick us up for a day or two. It was frustrating to know the narwhals were still swimming out there among the ice floes, far beyond our reach. How would we ever photograph them?

Next morning, as if by magic, the answer suddenly appeared. "John, look! It's an icebreaker!" There, rising majestically above the blue water of the bay, was the Canadian Coast Guard Ship *Franklin*. She must have slipped into Pond and dropped anchor sometime during the night. Of course, there was no way we could go whale-watching on such a big and powerful ship, but we knew that all icebreaking vessels carry their own helicopters. A scheme was already taking shape in our heads. Even before I turned away from the window, John was pulling on his boots and heading out the door.

The ship's helicopter came zooming in low over the water, heading for the airstrip to refuel. We raced through the village, tore up the hill and arrived, panting, just as the pilot was shutting down. Phase one of our scheme was to engage the pilot in friendly conversation. Phase two was to ask him to radio the ship's captain for permission to come aboard. (''Tell him we want to film his ship,'' I whispered in John's ear. Anything, I thought, just to get on board.) And how well our plan worked. Not only were we invited out to the ship, but it was ''with the compliments of the captain'' as well. Now, on to phase three.

The captain of the *Franklin* could not have been more courteous – or generous. He pressed us to have lunch on board, which we did (wishing we had something better to wear than our faded jeans. But we were here, after all, on assignment. They would just have to do). In the ship's dining room, surrounded by the smartly uniformed officers, we gradually steered the conversation to flying in general, and helicopters in particular. Then John turned to the captain and asked him, rather casually, if he...ah...ever let passengers fly in the ship's helicopter. One glance at our expectant faces, and at our cameras, must have told the captain what invitation we were angling for. His lips twitched and a slow grin spread over his face. ''Now just where might you be interested in going?'' he asked, innocently. We pointed to the sea and answered in unison, ''Out there.''

Within the hour, the chopper had lifted off from the deck of the icebreaker. It did not take us long to find the narwhals. Many were in small groups of three or four, but in one group I counted 18, all males. They lay quietly on the surface in a long line. The pilot quickly developed a technique for approaching the whales without scaring them. He slipped down very smoothly, flying his helicopter sideways. The whine of the chopper's turbine engine coming down from the sky did not seem to frighten the narwhals.

As I watched the narwhals moving through the still water below us, I thought of the early European explorers who had come to North America in wooden sailing ships centuries ago. How amazed they must have been by those long ivory tusks. Is that why they took home strange tales about a unicorn, a unicorn that lived in the sea?

People had always believed in the legend of the unicorn, a graceful horse-like creature with a white horn growing out of its forehead. The wondrous horn was said to be quite magical for it could detect the presence of poison. Since the kings and princes of the Middle Ages were surrounded by jealous, scheming rivals, they were only too willing to pay enormous sums in precious jewels and gold to buy the protection of the fabled unicorn's horn. But the horns that crafty merchants sold them came not from unicorns, but from narwhals. There is even a story that, in the 16th century, the king of Denmark's unicorn throne was made entirely from narwhal tusks.

Narwhals are not big by whale standards. Compared with a humpback whale, which is the size of a bus, a narwhal is more like a small sports car. And the tusk is not really a tusk, nor is it a horn. It is a left tooth that just grows...and grows....

There have been many theories about why the male grows such a long tusk. Some believe the narwhal uses it to stir up mud on the bottom and find food. Others think it uses it to break open breathing holes in the ice, or to spear codfish. We saw another use: two narwhals resting, their long tusks conveniently propped up on an ice floe, and holding them in place. Later we found out that males often use their long swords to spar with each other, fighting for dominance within the pod. Tips of tusks have been found embedded in the flesh of dead narwhals. Losing the tip of a tooth that long must be very painful. Imagine what a narwhal toothache must feel like!

Back and forth we flew across the inlet, tracking the whales as they moved westward past Pond Inlet on their summer journey. They were following migratory routes they have traveled for centuries. Today, a few of the puzzling questions about narwhals have been answered. Biologists have a better idea about where the whales have come from and where they are going as they travel through the Arctic. Yet no one knows for sure how many narwhals there are, or why they make their long journey every year. As one writer put it, "We know more about the rings of the planet Saturn than we know about narwhals."

In less than an hour we had seen 200 narwhals – and exhausted our film supply. We returned happily to the icebreaker, grateful to the ship's captain for allowing us such a rare opportunity to see the narwhals. Our mission to Pond Inlet was complete.

There is another small whale that also lives among the ice and embarks on long migratory journeys through the Arctic each summer – the white beluga. Unlike the narwhals, which spend their lives in high arctic waters, the belugas are also found farther south. Their comings and goings are more easily observed and much more is known about these first cousins of the narwhals. But still, there are mysteries. When we left Pond Inlet, we flew westward in the Twin Otter, seeking a solution to one of the white whale mysteries.

From high above the waters of Lancaster Sound, I peered through the small window of the aircraft and once again watched scattered ice floes drifting far below. The pieces of ice seemed to flow together, then dip and dive, stirring the water into waves and whitecaps. My mind snapped awake. Those were not ice floes. They were white beluga whales. More than 10,000 of them swim through Lancaster Sound each summer, following the same route as the narwhals into the High Arctic. And of those, about 1,000 head for Cunningham Inlet on the coast of Somerset Island. Why this deep bay with its many gravel bars is so attractive to the belugas has long been a mystery.

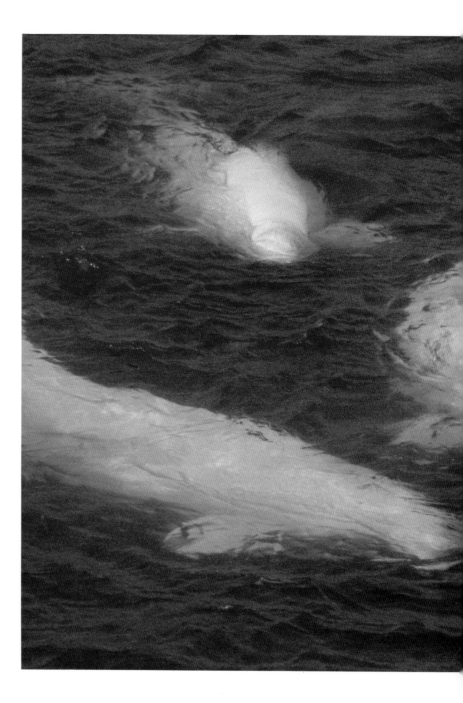

Soon after we bounced down on the gravelly plateau above the inlet, we met Tom Smith and Wybrand Hoek. They are marine biologists who spend entire summers here, living in tents, and watching and studying the belugas. Tom is trying to learn something about their language, for they really do talk to each other. These small whales are sometimes called "sea canaries" because they are the most vocal of all whale species, and they do have an amazing repertoire of sounds. In fact, we did not have to see the belugas to know they were in the bay, for the air was filled with their strange whistles, groans, mews and hisses. At times they sounded like babies crying, horses whinnying and even doors squeaking.

Twice each day, during the six hours of high tide, Tom climbs into his observation tower, bundles up in a thick parka and switches on a tape recorder. A long cable runs from the recorder to an underwater microphone that picks up the sounds the whales are making. At the same time, Tom is watching the whales and describing their movements into a second microphone. By listening to both tape tracks together, Tom is trying to learn what the belugas are ''saying'' as they turn, twist and dive.

Tom generously gave us the use of his tower so we could photograph the belugas during the next high tide. At low tide, we hiked out in our rubber hip waders across the gravel bars and climbed the steep ladder to the observation platform. When the tide turned, gradually rising and covering the gravel bars in the bay, the belugas came closer and closer until they were swimming right underneath us. The whales were shy, but curious. As they swam by, they would roll onto their sides and gaze up at us, or they ''spy hopped,'' floating vertically with their heads right out of the water and having a good look around. A young calf, closely following its mother like a pale shadow, passed below us. The mother was swimming so quickly that her calf was being pulled along in her slipstream. What an easy way to travel! From the tower, the calf seemed tiny, but it was at least 1.5 metres (5 feet) long.

We noticed something very interesting about the belugas. While many of them were gleaming white, others had patches of brown or yellow markings on their heads. We watched in puzzlement as a number of the whales swam into shallow water and wriggled about on the gravel bars, lifting their tails high in the air as they twisted and turned their smooth bodies. What on earth were they doing?

Back at camp that night, when we described the whales' strange behavior to Wybrand, he laughed. "Why," he exclaimed, "you've just seen the solution to the whale mystery of Cunningham Inlet." Each year, he told us, the belugas must molt their thin outer layer of skin. At the inlet, the fresh water from the Cunningham River mixes with the salt water, which helps to loosen that outer layer of skin. After three or four weeks of rubbing about on the gravel bars, the whales leave to continue their migratory journey, their new skin gleaming white. And that's why so many belugas visit Cunningham Inlet each summer – it's a good place to come for a scratch!

Breaking Through

We trudged down the long, gravelly beach, our boots scrunching noisily on the loose stones. There was a cold, knife's edge to the wind as it whistled past our ears. I shivered and hugged my jacket tighter. We were in sunlight, but out to sea dark storm clouds were bunching ominously on the horizon. Ahead of us, where the beach curved around the bay, we could see what we were searching for: three graves. They were little more than mounds of gravel covered with a few slabs of flat rock and large pebbles. In place of a tombstone, each had a rough wooden marker. I bent down and examined one but the lettering was so old and faded that I could barely make out the name: John Torrington, 1846. He was only 20 when he died. The lettering on the other two markers was impossible to read.

My gaze wandered over the island's bare hillsides, and out across the dark, ice-infested waters. What a bleak and desolate place to die. Poor John Torrington. Had he been filled with excitement and high expectations when he signed on with the Franklin Expedition in 1845 to discover the Northwest Passage?

Could he have known when the two wooden ships set sail from England that he would end his young life here, on Beechey Island's barren shoreline?

John and I had left the whales in Cunningham Inlet that day to fly across the Northwest Passage and land here, on Beechey Island, where Sir John Franklin and his men had spent the winter of 1845. And, incredible as it may seem, a wall of one of their buildings was still standing. From our reading, we knew it was part of a storehouse, constructed from beams and timbers taken from the ships. The crew had also built an observatory on the island, although we could find no trace of it. We did find stones carefully laid out and fashioned to make pathways. And farther up the hill were the remains of a small garden, now growing only lichens and mosses.

Franklin had come in search of the North-west Passage, the route through the arctic islands to the fabled riches of the Orient. For centuries, adventurous explorers – without the help of maps, compasses or charts – had searched in vain for the passage. Many died, the victims of ship-wrecks, exposure, scurvy or starvation. Henry Hudson's men grew tired of the fruitless search in 1611, and were so anxious to be home again in England that they cast their captain adrift in a rowing boat in the bay that now bears his name. Hudson was never seen again. Franklin's 1845 expedition was his third and he was convinced that this time he would find the Northwest Passage.

He set sail from England on May 19, crossed the Atlantic and had navigated westward through Lancaster Sound as far as Beechey Island by autumn. The expedition was off to a good start.

Franklin's men must have been fairly comfortable on Beechey Island that first winter. Just off shore, not far from where I now stood, their two sailing ships, the *Erebus* and *Terror*, were locked firmly into the ice. The journey was expected to take three years, and from the number of rusted cans we found lying on the ground, we guessed there had been no shortage of food. I held one of the small cans in my hand, turning it over and fingering the edges, still sharp after all these years, and I was reminded again that the Arctic is a dry, cold desert. Nothing rots or decays quickly. This is a land where some things can last forever.

How long the winter must have seemed for the crew, cut off as they were from the rest of the world. What did they do to escape the terrible boredom? We know the ship's library carried a large number of books and, no doubt, the officers would have organized games and special events to help fill the days. But how time must have dragged as they waited for spring. Looking around at the barren, empty landscape, I tried to imagine it in winter, with blowing snow, howling winds, months of darkness, and always the lurking danger of hungry polar bears.

During that first winter three of the seamen died. They were buried deep in the permanently frozen ground at the far end of the beach. One of them was the chief petty officer, John Torrington.

When the ice melted the following summer, releasing the trapped ships, the Franklin Expedition sailed away, never to be seen again. Two more years passed, and when there had been no sign of Franklin, a gigantic rescue operation was launched from England. Over the next 10 years, 32 expeditions came to the Arctic and searched for the lost explorer. But the area to be covered was so enormous, with so much of it unknown, that it was like looking for two ships lost in outer space. Lady Franklin herself outfitted two of the costly expeditions, and by the summer of 1850, there were 15 ships and 500 men combing the Arctic.

Over the years, piece by piece, the puzzle slowly came together. On King William Island, a long way south of Beechey, Inuit hunters told of a big boat that had sunk. They spoke of meeting half-starved white men who were falling and dying in their tracks. Some Inuit had silver spoons and forks that bore the Franklin crest; others had naval brass buttons. One group of searchers discovered a boat with the skeletons of two dead crewmen inside. Then, in 1859, one of the search parties found the last record of the Franklin Expedition. It had been written 11 years earlier:

April 25, 1848. Her Majesty's Ships Terror and Erebus were deserted on the 22nd April, having been beset since 12 Sept, 1846. The officer and crew consisting of 105 souls under command of Captain Crozier, landed here. Sir John Franklin died on the 11th June, 1847.

Captain Crozier and the 105 survivors had abandoned the doomed ships and struck out, on foot, across King William Island, hoping eventually to reach civilization. It was there that most of them died, their remains scattered over a stretch of coastline now called "Starvation Cove." It was a tragic end to Franklin's search for the Northwest Passage.

Today, there are many unanswered questions about the Franklin Expedition. Was it true the ships had not been so well provisioned, and that those empty cans we found on the beach had contained bad meat? Were the men on Beechey Island slowly starving that winter? Were they suffering from scurvy because of the lack of fresh fruit and vegetables? Was there any truth to the rumor that the crew were fighting among themselves? Had there been cannibalism? Were John Torrington and the other two seamen murdered? So many questions. . . .

A few years ago, a team of anthropologists flew here, to Beechey Island, and carefully dug up the grave of John Torrington. For close to 140 years his body had lain undisturbed, deep in the frozen ground. Imagine their surprise – and shock – when they reached the coffin and opened the lid. Instead of a mere skeleton, there was the full body of John Torrington, his frozen face staring up at them, eyes wide open. He had been perfectly preserved in the Arctic's deep freezer since the day he died.

The anthropologists spent four hours examining John Torrington and taking tissue samples. Then they reburied him. What did they learn? That the young seaman had not suffered from scurvy, nor had he been murdered. More likely, he had died of pneumonia. One small part of the Franklin mystery had been solved.

High on the cliff top overlooking their winter encampment, Franklin's men put up a tall marker, a ship's spar, with two biscuit barrels tied to the top. Had it been placed there to signal a passing ship, I wondered, or just to give the men something to do? I scrambled up the cliff and sat beside the spar, looking out over the sea, now sparkling with sunlight. What a strange twist there was to Franklin's tragic fate. If he had not gone missing, this region of unknown country might well have remained unknown for another 100 years. So many expeditions came looking for Franklin that, in the course of their searching, they mapped much of the Arctic. The Northwest Passage was finally discovered and much of the route was sailed. Franklin and his men, in their wooden sailing ships, had led the way.

How differently scientists and explorers travel among the arctic islands today. People rarely go missing, and ships don't become lost or trapped in ice for long. Science and technology have brought us a long way from the world of wooden sailing ships.

"Helicopter crew to flight deck. Helicopter crew to flight deck." The voice came crackling over the loudspeakers in the corridors of the Coast Guard Ship *John A Macdonald*. Quickly I left our cabin on the accommodation deck and, trying to remember where all the narrow connecting stairways were on the huge vessel, made my way down to the flight deck at the stern of the ship.

I arrived just as the Jet Ranger helicopter, painted in the red and white colors of the Canadian Coast Guard, was being wheeled out under the watchful eye of the officer in charge of the flight deck. I waited until he signaled I could come forward.

Standing in front of the helicopter were two "men from Mars." Dressed from head to foot in silver asbestos suits, each was armed with a long hose filled with foam. They were members of the fire team. Every time a helicopter lands or takes off from the deck of an icebreaker, the fire team is standing by, ready to handle any emergency.

Now the pilot and his passenger, the ship's ice observer, were climbing aboard the helicopter and preparing for takeoff. There was so much ice in Lancaster Sound that it was the ice observer's job to fly ahead and look for stretches of open water that would help the captain and navigator plot a quicker, easier course.

The chopper's big turbine engine whined into life and I turned away as the hurricane-force winds created by the spinning rotors swept the deck. Then the heavy machine was in the air, and away. It would be back to report within the hour.

John and I had joined the *John A Macdonald* in Lancaster Sound for a few days of photography and adventure on board the big ship. The *John A* is one of the largest icebreakers in the Canadian Coast Guard fleet. Her massive engines have 15,000 horsepower. Her hull has been specially reinforced with a wide strip of steel called an "ice band" to help protect the ship against the tremendous pressures and forces she encounters as she batters her way through the arctic ice. Today, the *John A* was going to have her work cut out for her.

On the bridge, Captain Gomes was not having an easy time. A short distance behind us, floundering and wallowing among great chunks of broken blue ice, was a cargo ship, the *Arctic Viking*. It was early in the summer shipping season, too early for the *Arctic Viking*. She was underbuilt and underpowered for the challenging conditions in Lancaster Sound and she was relying heavily on the Coast Guard icebreaker to help get her through.

The *John A* had already spent most of the morning breaking up the ice around her and clearing passageways through the thicker pans, but soon a small voice came over the loudspeaker on the bridge: "Captain, we're stuck again." Captain Gomes let out a small sigh as he quietly gave orders to bring the ship about. Back we went to break trail once more. Judging by the progress the *Arctic Viking* was making, this was going to be a very long day. "Should have named her the Arctic Turtle," I whispered to John.

How easily the *John A* moved. With her powerful engines at full throttle, the big ship drove ahead, her bow riding high as she plowed into the ice, the sheer weight of the ship cracking and breaking the floes apart under her. No wonder the hull had to be so strong. Great pans reared up and split apart in front of us like giant wedges of pie as we circled the *Arctic Viking*.

We cut trails on both sides of the cargo ship, then surged onward to clear out the forward passage, leaving behind us a wide trail of open black water filled with broken, shattered floes. Surely she can make it this time, I thought, glancing back at the *Arctic Viking*. But 10 minutes later came another cry for help. The cargo ship was unable to move through the chunks of ice that closed around her, blocking the channel and finally stopping her labored journey. What she really needed was a stronger hull and more powerful engines. Back we went again. Before long, I began to marvel at our captain's patience.

Captain Gomes was very much in charge of the operation. With his hand on the controls, he kept constant watch over the *Arctic Viking* from the rear windows and I was amazed at how carefully and precisely he could move the *John A* around her. From time to time he gave quiet orders to the quartermaster at the wheel to alter the ship's course, but mostly there were few words spoken. I had the feeling that, for the *John A Macdonald*, this was all in a day's work.

Meanwhile, the helicopter had returned, and the captain soon had the ice observer's report in his hands. Conditions ahead were not good. Captain Gomes was also studying aerial pictures taken moments before by a high-flying aircraft that is part of Canada's Ice Patrol. The pictures were taken by radar from above the clouds and transmitted electronically right to the bridge of the *John A*. They gave the captain a clear picture of the ice ahead. The patrol was also using laser beams to take surface profiles of the ice, revealing how thick and strong it was. In years to come, this work will be done by satellites circling the world, electronically scanning the globe 24 hours a day.

After two days on board the *John A Macdonald*, John and I had photographed the ship from stem to stern. What we really needed now were shots of the icebreaker "in action." But the only way to do that was for us to be down on the ice. We presented our problem to Captain Gomes one morning when the *Arctic Viking* seemed to be going even more slowly than usual. "Sure, we can put you down," he answered. "There's a long ridge ahead. We'll set you down out there." Noting the captain had said "we'll set you down," I naturally assumed we would be flying out by helicopter.

Leaving the *Arctic Viking* far behind, we steamed ahead until Captain Gomes found a particularly thick-looking ridge of old, multi-year ice.

Just as I was preparing myself for a helicopter ride, the ship's crew brought out the longest wooden extension ladder I had ever seen. And over the side we went, climbing down rung by rung. Looking up from the ice, we watched anxiously as our big camera was lowered to us on a rope. I prayed fervently that the crewman on top had a firm grip.

Captain Gomes steamed away, back to the *Arctic Viking*, and John and I were alone on the ice. Surrounded by the vastness and solitude of the Arctic, we suddenly felt very small. And then I remembered the polar bear tracks we had seen from the ship just the day before. Nervously, I checked out the ice all around us and carefully examined the line of dark hills in the distance. We could only hope the polar bear was well on into its journey and not likely to return. We set up our camera quickly, being careful to avoid the deep pools of melt water that lay on the surface, and focused on the *John A*, hard at work in the distance. When she came back for us, nearly an hour later, what a bright, welcoming sight she was against the white ice and the clear blue of the sky.

After another night and full day on board the icebreaker, we reached the edge of the pack ice. Ahead lay open water. The *Arctic Viking* could proceed on her own now and it was time for the *John A* to go to the aid of another supply ship in need of help. It was time for us to move on too. We had a plane to catch that would take us on to Resolute, in the middle of the High Arctic.

Resolute

High above the Northwest Passage, our 737 jet began a long, slow descent. The pilot was on his final approach to Resolute Airport on Cornwallis Island. We were coming in low over a bleak and rocky coastline. Below us telltale signs soon appeared on the gray landscape: tire tracks, rough roads and giant oil storage tanks. We were close to the settlement now. Somewhere ahead was the long gravel airstrip. Just before we touched down I glimpsed the shattered remains of two aircraft that had crashed years earlier while trying to land at Resolute in

fog. It was a grim reminder about the hazards of flying in the Arctic. I tightened my seat belt, thankful that today there was bright sun and blue sky.

We were coming in fast, as though the aircraft was tired of the journey and eager to be on the ground. As our wheels touched, a great storm cloud of dust billowed out behind and we roared down the runway, engines screaming and the plane vibrating so wildly I was shaking in my seat. We thundered by the passenger terminal, on past the parked Twin Otters and helicopters, the rows of fuel drums and pumps that make the big base look like a sprawling gas station. With flaps down and spoilers deployed, the pilot threw the big engines into reverse thrust to help break the jet's speed. Finally we slowed, and the friendly voice of the flight attendant came over the intercom, welcoming us to Resolute.

Nearly everyone who travels into the Far North comes first to Resolute. This is as far north as you can fly by commercial airline. From here on, it is strictly helicopter and Twin Otter country. In early summer Resolute is a very busy place, full of scientists and researchers – men and women heading out into the high arctic islands to begin their season's work. There were geologists and botanists on our flight. We hoped to see some of them again soon, at their high arctic campsites.

John and I collected our packs, boxes and camera cases, and made our way from the terminal building to the lodge where we would be staying for a few days. There we would have a chance to check over our gear before flying farther north.

Resolute sits on a flat tabletop of rocky land right in the middle of the High Arctic. But unlike other arctic towns and villages, the settlement doesn't have a long and colorful history. It was created, somewhat artificially, in 1947, when Canada and the United States agreed to set up a joint weather station and build an airstrip in the Arctic. They chose Cornwallis Island for their site and Resolute was born. By the 1950s, the search for oil and gas was under way and there were big plans for Canada's newest northern frontier.

The settlement at Resolute took shape quickly. Government buildings sprang up right beside the airstrip and many thought that one day Resolute would become a bustling northern metropolis. There were even plans for shopping malls and housing developments. The government spared no effort during these years to create an "instant community" on Cornwallis Island. Inuit families were persuaded to move to Resolute from other arctic villages and they settled in an area down by the water and away from the airstrip. Today, their village is home to the Inuit families that were moved here more than 30 years ago.

The Resolute base, with its complex of buildings and houses beside the airstrip, will probably never become the big town its developers dreamed of. But it is the transportation and communications centre for the whole of the High Arctic. Scientists camped at far distant points check in by radio twice a day with a base manager who answers them from a small cluttered office by the airstrip. He receives weather reports from all the distant camps, arranges camp moves and air flights, and relays important messages. The radio operator is an important link in the network, and the radio contact is like a safety line. In time of trouble, help will be on the way.

As John and I walked the dusty streets I couldn't help remembering how different Resolute had looked the last time we were here, just one year ago. It was late April then, early spring in most parts of southern Canada, but not in Resolute. True, the sun had returned after the long winter months of darkness and was shining 24 hours a day, but at midnight it hung very low and reluctantly on the horizon and the temperature hovered at a bone-chilling -29°C (-20°F). The days, while full of sunlight, were not much warmer. Every time the wind blew, I knew we were in the Arctic. And as we walked about half buried under layers of warm clothing and thick parkas, with eyes well goggled against the sun's glare, it was hard to feel very spring-like.

How white Resolute had looked then. The entire accumulation of winter's snow was still piled around the buildings. The RCMP offices were half buried and only the rooftop of the town cinema was peeking above the huge mounds. But the snow piles are deceptive. The High Arctic is a dry, cold desert. Less snow falls here in winter than in southern Canada or the northern United States. In fact, the High Arctic is even drier than the Sahara Desert. But the snow that does fall on Resolute blows and swirls around the buildings, packing itself into huge drifts that become rock hard. There the big drifts sit, without melting, until spring comes.

That April we had come to film three divers who were setting off to explore the fascinating underwater world. Diving here is very dangerous and only the most experienced will try it under the arctic ice. A dive hole had already been cut through the thick sea ice about a 20-minute run by snowmobile from Resolute. Inuit guides drove the snowmobiles and behind us we towed "komatiks" (big Inuit sleds with high sides) filled

with dive suits, lead weights, tanks of compressed air, metal boxes of film and a big, clear, waterproof box for Paul Mockler's camera. Paul is a filmmaker as well as a diver and he was going to record the underwater adventure.

When we reached the dive hole, we laughed, for it was already occupied by a young ringed seal. The Inuit told us its mother had probably been killed by a passing polar bear. The pup stayed on the ice with us, popping in and out of the dive hole. It seemed most interested in all the activity and when the divers began to suit up, the pup came right out of the water to watch.

The divers' bulky suits were made of tough, lightweight rubber. Under them they wore thick quilted underwear that created an insulated air space between their skin and the cold rubber to help keep them warm in the frigid arctic water. They could pump more air from their tanks into the air space to make an even better barrier against the cold, and give them buoyancy. Watching Paul and Barry dress up in their soft, woolly clothing, I had an idea we were going to be far colder standing around shivering above the ice than they would be swimming below it.

Now Paul and Barry were in the water, their compressed air hissing and bubbling in the hole behind them as they moved away under the ice. The seal pup had slipped down the hole just moments before and I wondered if they would all meet underwater. The third diver, Gary, stayed up on the ice, keeping a careful check on the divers below. He held the ends of their lifelines in his hands, playing them out like a fisherman, and always keeping a slight tension on the ropes so he could feel their movements. Inside each diver's helmet was a small microphone connected by a telephone wire to the surface. From under the ice the divers could communicate with Gary, and he could monitor their progress and judge their physical condition. Gary was also suited up in full gear. In an emergency, he would be ready to dive to the rescue.

The lifelines slackened, then tightened again as the divers headed for the bottom, so far below it was like diving to the bottom of an eight-story building.

The divers were under for no more than 20 minutes on their first dive, but for John and me it seemed more like an hour. I was filled with curiosity. What had they seen? What was it like?

''Amazingly clear,'' answered Paul, when he was back on the surface. The water was full of life. They had filmed beautiful jellyfish, and right on the bottom there were clams, crabs and small fish. The young seal pup had come up to Paul underwater and stared curiously into his face mask.

Then it had swum up to breathe the air in Paul's bubbles, which were trapped under the ice!

How incredible, to think of so much life in water so cold it could kill you in minutes if you fell in without a dive suit.

In spring, when sunlight comes back to the Arctic, the sea ice is just like a window letting in light to the darkness below. Plants need light to grow and below the surface, on the underside of the ice, a community of tiny plants – algae – begins to flourish. The plants soon attract small shrimp-like creatures called amphipods, which come to graze on these lush green pastures. Then, codfish will feed on the amphipods, their basic food. In turn, the cod will be taken by seals and, finally, the seals will be killed by polar bears. It is an interconnected chain of life, linking amphipods to polar bears. Paul was able to film the tiny amphipods by walking upside down under the ice, like an astronaut.

Just as the divers were preparing to go below again, one of our Inuit guides yelled and pointed. Far in the distance, beyond one of the long ice ridges, was a polar bear. I strained my eyes and could barely make out a big white shape appearing, then disappearing, behind the ridge. It seemed to be slowly moving away from us. Thinking we would want a good close-up picture, our guide leapt on the snowmobile and roared off in hot pursuit. "Please don't chase it!" we shouted, but it was too late. We scrambled for our cameras.

Through binoculars I could see the bear clearly. Already it was running, swinging its massive head from side to side and looking back, as though searching for an escape route from the noisy machine. Polar bears don't like snowmobiles. They associate them with gunshots and hunting season.

The snowmobile was now cutting a wide circle around the bear, trying to head it off. For a moment, the bear wheeled about, as though undecided, and then it began to run again – this time straight at us!

It was all happening so quickly there was no time to think. One minute the polar bear seemed to be a safe distance from us and the next moment we found ourselves standing right in its path. We had a gun for protection against bear attack but we did not want to use it. Quickly, we jumped into the komatik, hoping the bear would be too busy to pay attention to us.

The bear was closing the distance fast. Mouth wide open and breathing hard, it was now only seconds away. It paused suddenly in its wild dash and stared at us. For a moment that seemed to go on forever, I was eyeball-to-eyeball with the Lord of the Arctic.

We froze, not daring even to breathe. Then the bear thundered on by. Just ahead was a wide lead in the ice. Without hesitation the bear flung itself at the open water, breaking the smooth surface with a tremendous splash, and swam to the far side.

As the bear climbed back out onto the ice, it stopped and looked at us once more, water streaming from its fur. Perhaps now it felt safe, separated from us and the noisy snowmobile by deep, black water. Then, effortlessly, the bear broke into a run. Soon it was no more than a small speck in the distance, alone in its vast, icy, arctic world.

The memory of that close encounter with the polar bear was so sharp and vivid that it was hard to drag myself back to the present, and back to Resolute. But as John reminded me, we had packing and repacking to do. North of Resolute there would be no towns, hotels, restaurants or stores. From here on, everything we needed would be coming with us. We had just one day and not much time left to stock up on any last-minute supplies. I'd have to move fast if I wanted to grab a few of those chocolate bars I had seen in the store, before it closed.

An Arctic Oasis

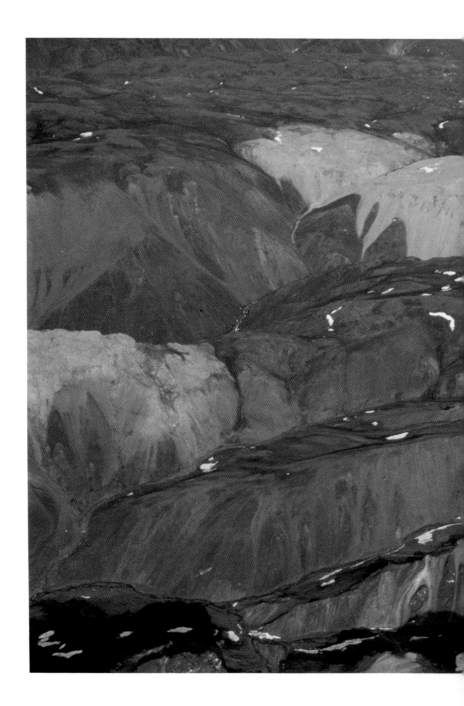

Next morning, right after breakfast, we hauled our packs over to the airstrip and added them to the small mountain of gear that our pilot, Duncan Grant, was loading into the Twin Otter aircraft. The fuel tanks had already been topped up for the long flight north and now Duncan was busy checking to make sure the aircraft would not be overloaded. There were four other passengers coming on our flight, plus all their belongings, and a heavy drum of extra fuel that Duncan had stowed on board for the long journey. Fortunately, the Twin Otter can easily carry a ton.

Soon we were squeezed into the narrow seats, with camera cases wedged tightly under our knees. The turboprop engines whistled and whined into life and the Twin Otter taxied smoothly into position at the end of the long gravel runway.

From my seat I could see Duncan talking through his headset to the air base control but it was impossible to hear much above the noise. Then we were off, roaring down the runway with the engines at full throttle. In seconds, we were airborne and gaining altitude fast.

We settled back, for it was going to be a long, four-hour flight, and carefully examined the large map spread out on our laps. A circle marked our first destination, an arctic oasis on Axel Heiberg Island.

How cold and hostile everything looked, and how empty. Gazing down on the bare hillsides, with their deep gullies still filled with last winter's snow, I wondered how anything managed to live in such a harsh environment. In a land so bleak, where could one hope to find an oasis? Once again I was reminded that much of the Arctic is a cold desert. And yet, the landscape had a rugged, awesome beauty. In places the mountains were so delicately tinted in soft shades of mauve, pink, brown and tan that we seemed to be flying across an oil painting. Long lines of snow ran like white threads through the valleys, dividing and separating the different shades of muted color.

The hours sped by as we flew farther and farther north. The distances were enormous, and I began to understand for the first time how vast the Arctic really is. Here there were no towns, no villages, no signs of any people, and our aircraft seemed tiny, and very insignificant.

The High Arctic can be dangerous flying country. Weather is changeable and unpredictable. Pilots must cope with frequent "whiteouts" when mountaintops and ice fields become hidden in cloud. But with Duncan we were in good hands. He knows the Arctic well from the air, knows its changing moods, its challenging terrain, its mountain peaks — and safe landing spots. And there is no better flying machine than the Twin Otter. It is a STOL (short takeoff and landing) aircraft. Ours was equipped with big wheels from a DC-3 aircraft. Their fat, soft tires are called "tundra tires" and they help absorb the shock of impact as the aircraft lands on beaches, gravel bars and even flat mountain plateaus. The Twin Otter is the perfect aircraft for the Arctic, and has really earned its name, "workhorse of the North."

If pilots get lost in the High Arctic, they can't use a compass to give them direction, for they are flying too close to the North Magnetic Pole. The compass cannot be trusted. But, as we quickly learned from Duncan, there are other ways to find direction in the High Arctic.

As soon as Duncan had gained altitude after leaving Resolute, he punched the precise position of the townsite into a small computer mounted on the instrument panel, locking the figures into the computer's memory. Also being fed into the computer were signals coming from ground stations throughout the Arctic. Instantly, the computer compared these incoming signals with the figures Duncan had punched in, and matched them against wind direction, air and wind speed, time and distance. It all sounded very complicated when Duncan first explained it to us but it means that right in front of him, on the instrument panel, is a constant visual display that lets him know if he is flying to the left, or right, of his chosen course. For Duncan and all the other pilots who fly the North, the computer is like a long string, guiding them out and bringing them safely home again. Still, Duncan was taking no chances. Once he had set course for Axel Heiberg, he peered through a strange device that looked like an ancient sextant mounted right in front of the windshield. It was a sun compass. Duncan was using a very old navigational technique: taking his position from the sun, then double-checking it against the computer!

Just as I was beginning to wonder how much farther we had to go, Duncan reached out and tapped my knee, beckoning me into the cockpit. ''There it is,'' he shouted into my ear, ''straight ahead of us.'' I looked to where Duncan was pointing and stared in utter amazement.

The entire valley floor was a vivid, startling shade of green. From the air, it looked like a giant golf course. But just as we were drawing closer, and I was leaning over his shoulder for a better view, Duncan banked the Twin Otter sharply away. I looked at him questioningly. "Muskoxen," he yelled. "Don't want to scare 'em." Sure enough, I could just make out a scattering of tiny dark shapes on the carpet of green. "I'll try to set you down somewhere behind those hills. You'll have to walk a bit, though."

On a second pass, Duncan found a clear strip of ground that was long and level enough for the Twin Otter and down we came, bouncing as the wheels touched. John and I piled out quickly and unloaded our packs. The other passengers were flying on to points farther north and Duncan had no time to waste. "Pick you up tomorrow," he shouted from the cockpit window, and then they were up, and away. The whine of the engines echoed and died in the distance, and we were enveloped in the silence of the Arctic.

It was now early afternoon. There was no time to put up our tent, not if we wanted to find the muskoxen. We grabbed a sandwich and, leaving our gear on a high ridge, set out across the valley.

The grasses under our feet were thick and luxuriant. It did not take us long to figure out why. The valley was warm, for it was a true arctic "thermal oasis," and high on one of the sheltering hillsides a long ridge of winter snow was melting in the bright summer sun.

Water seeped down into the valley 24 hours a day. In the Arctic, where there is water, there is life. Because of the icy barrier of frozen earth called permafrost lying just under the surface, the water can't escape but stays up in the thin soil, nourishing a carpet of grasses, tiny plants and mosses. And, we soon discovered, it also forms stagnant pools that are perfect breeding grounds for hordes of hungry mosquitoes!

We hiked . . . and we hiked. By four o'clock, my backpack felt so heavy it might have been filled with rocks, my boots were soaked through and I was bone tired. And still there was no sign of the muskoxen. Where had they gone? From the air, the valley had looked so much smaller. Our eyes were beginning to play tricks on us, for after three exhausting hours of hiking we were not even halfway across, and the muskoxen had vanished. "Come on," John called back, "let's keep going. They could be tucked in behind those hills on the right." Muttering under my breath, I eased the shoulder straps of my pack, tightened the waist belt and trudged on after him, batting at the clouds of mosquitoes that persisted in traveling with us.

And suddenly, there they were, just beyond the hill. Grouped tightly together, shoulder to shoulder, the animals stood facing us in a half circle. I counted six or seven of the shaggy beasts.

Easing the tripod out of my pack, I quickly mounted a long lens on the camera. There was no telling how the animals would react to our presence and, remembering that they can run like the wind, we stayed well back.

The muskoxen were surprisingly small. In photographs, with their huge heads and shaggy coats, they seem as big as buffalo. But, in fact, they stand only half as tall, and their nearest cousins are sheep and goats. Muskoxen have good hearing, keen eyesight and a sharp sense of smell. In winter, they use their massive heads like snowplows to clear away the surface snow, then paw down through the frozen crust with their hooves to reach the vegetation below. In bad years, when rain comes late in the fall, the icy crust can become too thick and many muskoxen may die from starvation.

The muskox is one of the few large animals to have survived the Ice Age, and it is well adapted to the harshness of the arctic environment. Under its long coat is a thick, inner layer of soft wool called "qiviut" that is eight times as warm as sheep's wool, and just as strong. The Latin name for muskox means "sheep like cow with musky smell," but the name the Inuit gave it, Oomingmag, paints a far better picture — "the animal with skin like a beard."

Now the herd grew restless. A wind blew across the valley, carrying our scent. Breaking formation, the frightened animals galloped away, their long woolly skirts rippling like curtains.

For a moment they looked like Stone-Age rock paintings that had come to life. Then they were gone.

There are not many thermal oases in the High Arctic and I wondered how far the herd had traveled to reach this one. Muskoxen, caribou and arctic hare depend on the rich vegetation for survival, particularly during the cold months of winter. On our way back to camp we passed the carcass of a muskox. Perhaps it had died of old age, or been killed by an arctic wolf. Now, only the horns and bones were left, and a few tufts of muskox wool caught up in some tiny pink flowers. In time, the bones would break down and become a little bit of fertilizer for the arctic tundra. As we walked by, a small bird fluttered down, picked up a tiny ball of muskox wool and flew off with it. John laughed. ''I bet she's using it to line her nest.''

That evening we sat high on the hillside and gazed out over the valley, marveling once more at the beauty of an arctic oasis. Then, just before crawling into the tent, I spotted something white on the sea of green. It was an arctic wolf, coming into the oasis to look for food. Perhaps, like us, it was searching for the muskoxen.

We set out next morning to explore more of the valley but had not gone far when we almost tripped over a big bull muskox. Just the top of his woolly head was showing above the deep gully he was standing in, and it blended in perfectly with the arctic tundra.

He grunted once or twice, but otherwise didn't seem disturbed by our sudden arrival.

Muskoxen live in small herds during the summer and group up into larger herds for the winter. This muskox seemed to be living by himself. Perhaps he had been forced out of the herd by a more aggressive male, or maybe he simply preferred to live alone.

Once again we dug out our cameras, scarcely believing our good fortune at finding ourselves so close to a muskox. I wondered, fleetingly, if he would be frightened or angered by our presence, but the bull seemed far more interested in the side of the gully than he was in us. He kept butting it with his long, curved horns and tearing out large chunks of earth. Occasionally, he would stop butting and rub the side of his front leg with his head. Fascinated with this interesting behavior, we kept right on photographing. What we did not know was that the muskox was sending us body language signals. From a small gland located just below his eye, the male muskox was secreting a strongly scented oil and rubbing it on his front leg. Had John and I been other male muskoxen, we would have smelled the musky odor and recognized the signal: "Get away. You are too close!"

Not knowing muskox body language, we stayed where we were. But then John decided to try for a different camera angle. He walked around to the other side of the deep gully so that the bull was between us. And for the muskox, that did it.

He turned and charged. John, in panic, leapt over the bank behind him (to me, it was more like flying than leaping) and fell flat on his face in a pool of icy-cold water. Scrambling up out of the water, he looked up to see the muskox on the ridge above him, grunting deep in his throat.

The muskox had given John a "false charge." It was a clear warning to us and we didn't wait to get another. Retrieving our packs from where we had dropped them, we made a very hasty retreat under the glaring eyes of the muskox, who watched our every move. Later, we learned that solitary bulls have a reputation for being irritable and cantankerous. But for me, the image of John scrambling up the bank, soaking wet, was the highlight of our adventure in the oasis — although John has rather different feelings about that particular highlight!

Late at night, with the sun still bright in the sky, Duncan came back for us, the Twin Otter whispering so quietly into the valley that we scarcely heard it until he was circling overhead. We were packed and ready to go but as we boarded the aircraft, I stopped and looked back, reluctant to leave this warm and sheltered green valley. And I wondered if we would be lucky enough to find another oasis as big and as beautiful as this one in the vast desert of the High Arctic.

The ～ Land from Somewhere Else

You mean that was once a tree?"

I stared in wonder at the chunk of heavy gray rock nestled in Dave's arms.

"That's right," Brian answered, "and not just any tree, but a tropical sequoia. It's millions and millions of years old. In fact, it's so ancient that the wood has become fossilized and turned into rock."

Brian rolled the rock over and held it up to the sunlight, tracing its surface with his finger. "Look at those lines and patterns. You can see where the bark was. There's no doubt about it. That stump was once part of a big tree."

I ran my hand lightly over the rock, recognizing the wood grain and trying to visualize the living sequoia, a tree that might easily have grown to a height of 49 metres (160 feet).

Tropical sequoias? Growing here in the barren landscape of Axel Heiberg Island? It seemed so unlikely. Then I had to remember that millions of years ago this island looked very different.

In fact, 350 million years ago, Axel Heiberg wasn't even here.

Brian's assistant, Dave Allen, shows us the fossilized stump of an ancient sequoia.

62

But where was it? And how did it get here? The answer lies in the fascinating theory of "continental drift."

Between 300 and 400 million years ago, all the world's continents were clustered together in one giant land mass that scientists call "Pangea," a Greek word meaning "whole earth." The crust of the earth, the land we stand and live on, is actually very thin. Try thinking of our planet as an egg or, better still, a hard-boiled egg. The eggshell is the earth's thin outer crust. The white of the egg is a thick layer of dense rock called the earth's mantle and the yolk is the center of the planet, a bubbling cauldron of hot, molten lava. Sometime in that far distant past, perhaps 350 million years ago, the fiery, white-hot interior generated so much heat and pressure that Pangea's thin outer crust, the "eggshell," began to crack and fracture into pieces. South America broke apart from Africa and began to drift away. India became separated from Asia, and North America from northern Europe. If you study a map you can see how well the world's continents once fitted together.

When Pangea broke apart, the part of the eggshell that would become the arctic islands was on the same latitude as present-day Florida. At that time, it would have been covered in lush tropical forests. Then it began to move northward, sliding over the molten rock below. It traveled very, very slowly, no more than a few centimetres a year. The long journey lasted hundreds of millions of years — and continues today.

Axel Heiberg Island is, indeed, a land from somewhere else.

But Brian's fossilized stump did not come from somewhere else. That stump was part of a living sequoia tree that was growing right here, in the middle of the Arctic, 45 million years ago.

No one knows why, but the world's climate was much warmer then. Perhaps it was because of all the earthquakes and volcanoes that were erupting as the continental plates moved about the globe. So much dust and carbon dioxide would have been released into the earth's atmosphere from the volcanoes that they might have blanketed the earth and created a "greenhouse" effect in the Far North. It was so warm then that the Arctic Ocean did not freeze, even in winter. It's hard to imagine these same windswept arctic islands 45 million years ago covered, not with sparse mosses and lichens, but with lush forests of huge redwoods and giant sequoia trees.

Dried wood from a tree that lay buried for millions of years.

And it's even harder to imagine alligators, snakes, exotic butterflies, giant tortoises and all sorts of strange and wonderful creatures living here in warm tropical swamps. I shook my head. I was going to have to change my whole way of thinking about the Arctic.

But now, back to the present.

John and I were at Strand Fiord, on the coast of Axel Heiberg Island. We were camped with a large group of friendly, talkative and enthusiastic geologists who know a great deal about the way the earth was formed and how the land moved about. It was very late when we arrived but the whole camp was gathered in the big cook tent. Dinner hour was over. Empty plates had long since been pushed aside and around the table there was lively conversation, animated debate and heated discussion. In no time at all our minds were being filled with new ideas, theories and speculations about the move-ments of the continents and the long geographical history of the High Arctic.

Brian Ricketts is a volcanologist, searching for large beds of coal that would have come from those ancient, decaying forests. That's how he stumbled across his fossilized sequoia tree. Ashton Embry and Jack Macmillan are sedimentologists. They were here examining sedimentary rock, the solidified mud from ancient seas and rivers. There was also a paleontologist in camp who was collecting the fossils in the ancient rock formations. And lastly, there was Ted Irving, who has spent most of his life studying magnetism in the earth.

Ted's field, paleomagnetism, is almost as difficult to understand as it is to pronounce. But slowly and patiently he tried to explain it to us. The earth's North Magnetic Pole, the direction our compasses always point to, has moved and changed position throughout the earth's history. But the rocks contain a magnetic record of where it was in the past.

Ted Irving (left) and his assistant extract a core sample from the rock in order to study the earth's magnetism.

"Think of the rocks as little frozen compasses," Ted instructed us, as he moved the salt and pepper shakers on the table to represent a rock and the North Magnetic Pole. "The iron elements in the rock were magnetized by the earth's magnetic field millions of years ago, when the liquid rock cooled and hardened."

Today, those same iron elements, still frozen deep inside the rock, point to where the North Magnetic Pole was *at that time*, hundreds of millions of years ago. By using very precise instruments and tools, Dr. Irving can drill into the rock and extract a piece that contains the memory, the record, of where the North Magnetic Pole was when the rock was formed.

By now my head was beginning to spin. Volcanology, paleontology, sedimentology, paleomagnetism, there were so many descriptions and explanations — and new words — that I could hardly keep them all straight. And it was the middle of the night!

"Don't geologists ever go to bed?" I whispered to John, as we slipped out quietly to set up our tent.

There were so many tents clustered together on the cliff above Strand Fiord that the geologists' base camp looked like a little tent city. We pitched ours near the edge of the cliff, which gave us a grand view of a grounded iceberg in the middle of the saltwater fiord. A fast-flowing river was surging out of the distant mountains behind us. One of its channels ran right under our cliff top, so I scrambled down the steep slope to fill up our water containers. But the river was carrying such a heavy load of silt picked up on its journey down from the mountains that the water looked like liquid mud.

What did the geologists do when they were thirsty, I wondered, as I climbed back up to the tent. They certainly couldn't drink the brown, sandy river water, and the fiord was too salty.

Early next morning, the puzzle was solved. I awoke to the sound of a helicopter. A long cable was suspended under the chopper and dangling from the end of it was a large, empty steel drum. I watched, mystified, as the helicopter flew out with its strange load and then hovered above the iceberg. The pilot lowered his chopper until the drum swinging at the end of the cable disappeared right into the heart of the iceberg. What on earth was the helicopter doing?

Moments later, it came whining back into camp. The steel drum was full of clean, clear fresh water that had been scooped up from a basin of melt water trapped in the iceberg. That iceberg, which had drifted into the bay from a nearby glacier, was providing the geologists with an endless supply of water. And as the glacier had come from the last ice age, the melt water was very, very old.

John grinned delightedly. "Just think," he said, "the geologists can sip ancient water while they study ancient rocks!"

Sharing meals with the geologists made a welcome change from our rations of freeze-dried food. At breakfast time the big dining tent was a lively place, full of chatter and wonderful smells. There is nothing like starting a day in the Arctic with a big bowl of porridge, crispy bacon and eggs, buttered toast that fairly drips with honey, and pots of hot tea.

Every day, small groups of geologists headed out, either on foot or by helicopter, to begin their day's work. John and I were invited to fly out with Ashton and Jack. Their work site was up in the mountaintops nearby, where they were studying sedimentary rocks. These mountains on Axel Heiberg used to be the bed of an ancient sea. As we flew among them, I noticed wide bands of dark rock. Ashton leaned over and yelled in my ear, "That's shale. Used to be mud at the bottom of the sea before the mountains were pushed up."

We landed on a high mountain plateau. With small geological hammers that have picks in one end, Jack and Ashton chipped out samples of rock from the dark-colored shale and packaged them in clear plastic bags. Much later, the samples would be carefully examined under microscropes for grains of pollen from ancient vegetation and tiny microfossils left by the creatures that lived and died in the Arctic's warm tropical seas and swamps. Over millions of years, squeezed under great layers of silt and sediment, that organic matter might well have been converted into oil or gas. But, as Jack admitted, nothing is certain. Rock is very porous and the oil can escape.

"We could predict where the oil should be," Jack explained, "but by the time the oil companies drilled for it, the oil might have vanished."

"Luck," added Ashton, "you need a lot of luck."

Geologists need a lot of patience too, I thought, as we watched them go carefully about their work. Jack and Ashton would have to live for millions of years to really see how mountains are pushed up and layers of sediment formed.

Biologists and zoologists are much luckier; they can watch their living subjects grow, develop and change all in one season. And in other camps throughout the High Arctic this summer, there were biologists doing just that — examining bird colonies, closely observing sea mammals and counting wildlife population numbers. If large supplies of oil and gas are ever found here, the development and transportation of those resources might have a very serious effect on the Arctic's wildlife. The more scientists know about the fragile arctic environment, the better we'll all be able to protect it.

By the time we headed back to camp, Jack and Ashton seemed well pleased with their day's work. Tomorrow they would collect samples from a different area. Like important pieces of a jigsaw puzzle, the small rock samples would one day give them a much clearer picture of the island's geological history.

In geology, where things happen so slowly, there can also be sudden and unexpected drama. Just recently, as I was sitting down to write this book, an exciting discovery was made on Axel Heiberg Island.

Brian had been out searching for coal deposits when he came across an area covered with dried tree stumps from ancient tropical forests. They were amazingly well preserved. Unlike the rock-hard, fossilized stump he had shown us, these had been buried so deep and for so long that they were dried, or mummified. The wood could be cut with a saw or ax, and even burned. There were more than 200 stumps on one site and some of them measured two metres (6 feet) across. The once living trees must have been giants. James Basinger, a paleobotanist who studies ancient vegetation, was very excited by the discovery. "You can see a prehistoric forest," he said, "how dense it was, how the trees grew." He found 19 different layers of stumps buried underground. Each layer was a forest that developed, lived for centuries and then died. The ancient pine cones and leaves found at the site looked so fresh they could have been 45 instead of 45 million years old. For scientists, it was like finding pure gold.

Jane Francis is an expert on fossil forests. This stump was once a tree that grew 40 to 65 million years ago.

On our last night in camp, we sat once more around the big table in the dining tent listening to the scientists talk about their different projects with excitement and enthusiasm. In the High Arctic, there are still so many unanswered questions, so many unsolved riddles about the mountains, the rocks and the earth. How could one ever hope to learn the truth about what happened millions and millions of years ago?

Then, from the far end of the table, one of the geologists told us how he explained the search for geological truth to his students:

"I think of nature," Phil Simony said, "as a mother, a kindly mother — Mother Nature. And the way to find things out is the way a child finds things out from a wise mother. If you sit on her lap, and ask the right questions, she'll give you some answers, but the answers don't always lead directly to the next step. You have to keep asking, and eventually you get closer and closer to the truth, or the cookie jar. I think of studying the earth the same way. You ask the right kind of questions: you sit on her knee, you listen carefully, and you do eventually find out where the cookie jar is hidden."

As we bade farewell next morning to Brian and Phil, and to Ashton and Jack, I could only hope that their summer here at Strand Fiord would lead them a little closer to that elusive cookie jar.

Alexandra Fiord

Hang on to your hats!'' Duncan shouted as he circled low over the fiord, easing back on the throttle to bring the Twin Otter in for a tight landing. Of all the places to set down in the High Arctic, the short strip of lumpy ground that serves as a runway at Alexandra Fiord on Ellesmere Island must be the very worst. There's a pile of rocks at one end of the strip, a flowing stream at the other, and a big bump right in the middle. That bump always tries to bounce the plane back into the sky just when the pilot is trying to stay on the ground. Landing at Alexandra Fiord is a real test of a pilot's skill. It's a good test of a passenger's nerves too, I thought, burrowing into my seat as the ground came rushing up to meet us.

Bump...bounce...and we were down, roaring across the tundra with everything on board shaking and rattling. I grabbed a small pack just in time as it skidded out from under a seat and went flying down the aisle. The plane lurched violently as we hit the big bump in the middle of the runway but the wheels stayed on the ground and we came to a shuddering stop.

By the time we had unloaded the aircraft and found a place to pitch the tent it was two o'clock in the morning. Behind our camp, a long green valley rolled away to meet the gigantic tongue of a glacier flowing out from the distant mountains. And all around us were tall mountain peaks. Late as it was, I couldn't wait to explore our surroundings. Leaving John to finish the unpacking, I headed for the beach.

Alexandra Fiord was once the most northerly post of the Royal Canadian Mounted Police. The police force abandoned the base a long time ago but five or six small white wooden buildings still stand clustered on the shoreline overlooking the sea. In front of one of the deserted houses was a small rock garden filled with clumps of blooming yellow arctic poppies planted by the families who once lived here.

How peaceful and quiet Alexandra Fiord was, and how bright. The sun hung low on the horizon, casting such a perfect reflection in the still water of the fiord that there were two suns sparkling, one in the sky and one on the sea.

Alexandra Fiord, we learned to our delight, was another thermal oasis. Imagine a wide, sheltered valley that is enclosed by a dazzling white glacier at one end, a bright sparkling sea at the other, and high, steep rock walls on both sides. These are Alexandra Fiord's natural reflectors. On clear summer days and nights, bright sunlight pours like golden honey into the valley 24 hours a day. It reflects off the sea, the ice and the rock. With so much radiant light and heat coming into the valley, the temperature on the valley floor can be as much as six or seven degrees higher than in all the surrounding areas. No wonder we were soon shedding our bulky parkas and hiking in just our shirt sleeves!

The tundra beneath our feet was a carpet of tiny flowers, all in full bloom. Arctic plants have a hard time growing, even in thermal oases. The soil is good but it's thin and dry, and the underlying layer of permafrost always keeps the ground cool, even in summer. Arctic tundra can also be scarred easily, and once damaged, it takes a long time to recover. We tried to be very careful around camp but our hiking boots still left trails that marked our comings and goings. In the Arctic, the tracks left by a heavy bulldozer can last a hundred years.

The growing season is very short. Summer lasts just six weeks, so plants don't have much time to flower and set seed. Even in July there can be sudden snowfalls or fierce cold winds that come sweeping down the mountains and over the glacier to chill the valley floor.

Living in such a harsh climate, plants have had to develop special ways to help them survive and flourish. They don't grow very tall, but hug the ground, seeking whatever warmth there is in the soil. We found heather, poppies, lupins, and even tiny buttercups in the High Arctic, but unlike their tall cousins in the south, these were all dwarf size. The arctic willow, for example, is the closest plant there is to a tree in the High Arctic. But instead of growing upright into the air like a normal tree, it very sensibly stays low and spreads itself out over the ground like a long, wandering vine. Other plants, like the purple saxifrage and moss campion, bunch themselves tightly together in wide round roseates to gain some protection from the wind. And the blossoms of the arctic poppy have learned to track the sun on its journey like little yellow satellite dishes, capturing all the heat they can. Inside the flowers of the arctic poppy, the temperature will be a few degrees warmer so a passing bumblebee will be persuaded to stop and linger awhile. And so the poppy will be pollinated.

What a surprise it was to find fat bumblebees in the High Arctic! In winter, they hibernate under the snow, their bodies creating a form of antifreeze that keeps them alive until spring. And a little butterfly fluttered past my left ear while I was down on hands and knees photographing the flowers.

But we were soon in for an even bigger surprise. On the tundra was a large painted sign that read "Green Igloos," and behind it was a girl waving with one hand and clutching a plastic watering can in the other. "Come and see my gardens," she called out. Gardens? In the High Arctic?

Halfway up the valley there were indeed gardens — and greenhouses, or "green igloos," as they were called. Jenny Hale is a botanist and she was here at Alexandra Fiord with a small group of researchers conducting an experiment in high arctic gardening. Taking advantage of the summer sunlight 24 hours a day, and the added warmth of a thermal oasis, they were trying to see how successfully they could grow potatoes.

In the first garden plot Jenny showed us, the potatoes were protected only by a small fence made out of clear plastic to help cut down on the wind's force. "They're really slow," Jenny admitted. "We're not giving these ones any fertilizer, just water. They are getting lots of sunlight but they have a long way to go."

Jenny guided us to a second garden plot. "These are doing much better," she said. Here the plants were not only protected by a little fence but also by a blanket of clear plastic placed right over the rows. The plastic mulch helped keep the warmth and the moisture in the ground and the dark green leaves poking through were much larger. Jenny was giving these potato plants small amounts of fertilizer as well as water. Still, I couldn't help thinking it would be a long time before baked potatoes were served at Alexandra Fiord.

"But now," Jenny announced proudly, "come and see our real success story." Beyond the garden plots were a number of small greenhouses also made out of clear plastic. Jenny took us to the largest one, unzipped the wall and disappeared inside. We followed her and found ourselves stepping into another world, one that was warm, moist and full of greenery. I could scarcely believe my eyes. All around us were beans, trailing sweet peas, lettuces, Chinese cabbages, bushy potato plants growing in pots made of black plastic, and radishes as big and as red as ripe cherries. My mouth watered. I could almost taste them.

Jenny handed me a pot containing a large, leafy lettuce. "Just think, in an arctic village, that might cost you over $5." I remembered seeing the small selection of expensive vegetables available in the Resolute store. Flown up from distant farms in the south, none of them were that fresh either. It certainly made sense to grow produce right here in an arctic greenhouse under the constant summer sun.

We left Jenny to finish tending her gardens, but not before she had popped a big Chinese cabbage and a bunch of radishes into my pack to take back for our supper.

No sooner had we arrived at camp than we spotted another neighbor carefully threading his way between the ice floes in a small rubber boat. It was Peter Schlederman, an archaeologist who was busy excavating an ancient Thule Eskimo site on Skraeling Island, not far from

where we were camped. We quickly accepted his invitation to journey out to see the site, and piled right into his small craft.

It was a tight fit with all three of us squeezed into the rubber boat. Luckily there was no wind and the sea was smooth as glass but still, the voyage took a long time, almost an hour.

Often, we had to take long, circuitous routes around the huge ice floes that blocked our passage.

From a distance, Skraeling Island is a mound of bare rock rising up out of the sea. It was hard to imagine anyone camped here today, let alone hundreds of years ago. How cold and inhospitable it seemed. Peter's fellow workers helped us ashore and warmed us up with steaming mugs of hot chocolate before taking us to see where they were digging up the old Eskimo site.

Nearly a thousand years ago, a large community of Eskimos lived on Skraeling Island. They came from Greenland and were part of a very old culture called Thule, the name given to Greenland in ancient times. These distant ancestors of today's Inuit were a hunting people and probably settled on Skraeling Island because of the nearby polynya (an area of the Arctic Ocean that never freezes over, where seals, walrus and whales spend their winters). Even in the coldest months, it would have provided them with a good supply of walrus and seal meat. I stood on the edge of all that was left of one of their winter houses, a deep ditch dug down into the tundra to give the home some protection against the cold. Its roof would have been made from whale bone and covered with seal or caribou skins, just like the old house we had seen in Labrador. Peter could point out where the kitchen had been, the entrance tunnel and passageway, and even the different sleeping areas.

Digging out the ancient houses was not easy. The archaeologists could only dig down so far each day, then they had to wait for the ground to thaw so they could dig further. "And working in the kitchen area is the worst," Peter said, wrinkling his nose. "Even after hundreds of years, leftover smells of rotting seal meat can be pretty overpowering."

Peter and his group had been here most of the summer, searching for artifacts and clues buried deep in the permafrost from a long-ago people and an ancient culture. Using strong shovels first, then tiny trowels and brushes, they had uncovered more than 20 different house sites. It had been careful and painstaking work. But what amazing things they had found! Peter showed us pieces of ancient pottery, harpoon heads, decorated

ivory needle cases and beautiful pendants and ornaments, all carved from the tusks of walruses. One was in the shape of a snow goose; another might have been a loon.

They had found artifacts that were undoubtedly European in origin: bits of copper, sections of chain mail, and metal boat rivets. These might well have been trade goods. And Karen, Peter's assistant, showed me one of their most exciting finds. It was a small fragment of brown woollen cloth. I could see nothing to get excited about until Karen told me it was 700 years old and that from the pattern of the weave, they knew it was Norse in origin.

The Norsemen were adventurous explorers who set out across the Atlantic in their Viking ships a thousand years ago. They were the first Europeans to reach the North American mainland, and now it seems likely that they had come to the High Arctic, exploring and trading with the ancient Eskimo. Perhaps they had even come here, to Skraeling Island. It was that kind of evidence that Peter and Karen were searching for.

When Peter ferried us back to our camp, there was good news waiting. A radio message had come through from Duncan. Resolute was closed down by thick fog. Nothing was flying in or out of the base. From the sound of the forecast, the Twin Otter would not be heading up our way again for a day or two. I was delighted. We could not have planned a better place to be stranded in and there was still much to see and do before we left the valley.

A long morning's hike took us to the shining glacier at the head of the valley. Beside the stream of melt water that flowed away from the glacier, we encountered a mother ptarmigan and her large family. With her brown feathers, she blended in so well against the tundra that whenever she stood still, she disappeared. The chicks hopping along behind her were no bigger than tiny fluff balls and I kept losing them among the small rocks and boulders. But it was no trouble to pick out the ruddy turnstone with its bright,

rusty feathers and gaily colored orange legs. The little bird was doing just what its name said — flipping over small stones and pebbles in the stream to look for tasty insects.

I found our best photographic subjects the night I went down to brush my teeth in the cold water of the fiord. A small family of snow geese was crossing the ice floes on shore. The four goslings flapped their tiny wings mightily as they hopped from ice floe to ice floe, struggling hard to follow and keep up with their parents. By late August the family would be joining up with all the other snow geese in Canada's Eastern Arctic and migrating south to New Jersey and South Carolina, stopping to rest and feed in the salt marshes of the St. Lawrence. I remembered having seen them there once. There were so many thousands of birds that each time the flocks landed or took off, it was like a sudden blizzard of swirling snowflakes.

For our last night at Alexandra Fiord, Jenny and her teammates organized a lively, rousing game of volleyball under the midnight sun. There was so much laughter floating and echoing across the bay that I wondered what the snow geese thought of it all.

Top of the World

At last, we were finally winging our way up toward the tip of North America. I kept my face pressed to the small window of the Twin Otter, drinking in all the splendor and majesty of the land beneath us. Ellesmere Island is enormous, bigger even than Great Britain. Its mountains dominate the land and their peaks are among the highest on the eastern side of North America.

Duncan flew low through deep valleys between the long mountain ranges. We spotted scattered groups of muskoxen on the barren slopes, and occasionally a few caribou, but mostly the land seemed empty and deserted, a vast and awesome wilderness stretching endlessly northward.

A few hours later, we were circling over the sparkling blue waters of Tanquary Fiord. Duncan dropped the nose of the Twin Otter and we came in for a smooth, easy landing on the gravel airstrip.

We pitched our tent once more. Across from us, a long glacier hung from the mountaintop like a giant frozen tongue, and behind us, we could look into three winding green valleys and glimpse the high, snow-capped mountains beyond.

And we were not alone. While we unpacked, young arctic hare bunnies hopped and scampered about, nibbling the tiny flowers that carpeted the tundra and happily chewing the leaves of the arctic willow, their favorite food. They were very young, no more than three or four weeks old and not at all concerned about sharing their territory with us. Indeed, in the days that followed, they became quite accustomed to seeing us sneak up behind them on our hands and knees, with cameras clutched in our hands.

Tanquary Fiord was as far north as John and I had ever pitched our tent and to celebrate that first night I searched through our selection of freeze-dried food and chose one of the more exotic meals for supper — a cheese and nut casserole. Now to my eye, freeze-dried food always looks like a mixture of sawdust and wood chips when it comes out of the bag. But just add water and boil it for about 20 minutes and the mixture undergoes a magical transformation. Served up with freeze-dried peas and instant mashed potatoes, it made a delicious supper. And to mark the special occasion even further, for dessert we treated ourselves to two small squares of hard chocolate.

87

After supper we took steaming mugs of hot tea down to the water's edge and sat watching the evening's entertainment: a pair of arctic terns having a late-night bath in the fiord. Sparkling, silvery droplets flew in all directions from their wings, creating rainbows of light as the birds flapped about noisily in the shimmering water. Arctic terns are splendid long-distance travelers. Each year they migrate from the polar regions of the Arctic to the polar regions of the Antarctic, seeing more days of 24-hour sunlight in both winter and summer than any other bird on earth.

Just before crawling into the snug warmth of our sleeping bags, we tried an experiment. Taking the compass, John pointed it toward the sun, sitting low on the north horizon. It was exactly midnight and we knew the compass needle should have pointed north, toward the sun. But instead, the needle swung crazily round and round in a circle until it ended up pointing somewhere to the southwest. Now we knew beyond doubt that we were camped at the top of the world: Tanquary Fiord is farther north than the North Magnetic Pole.

Next morning, I woke up to the sound of raindrops hitting the soft sides of the tent. "How can it possibly rain?" I wailed, hearing the gentle pitter-patter turn into a torrential downpour. "This is supposed to be a cold, dry desert!" But of course it does rain in the Arctic, even in the High Arctic, and especially in the summer, when the sea ice melts and the open waters create thick fog banks.

We spent the morning around camp, checking our gear and writing up the diary. By lunchtime the rain had let up enough for us to boil soup and cook a bannock over the stove. The sweet, tantalizing smell of moist bread frying in the pan soon brought in five hungry long-tailed jaegers. One of the birds perched boldly right on top of the tent, waiting for free handouts. The other four hung on the wind above us, cleverly swooping down to catch in their beaks small pieces of the bannock that I tossed up to them. From that moment, the jaegers became our constant dinner companions, never missing a meal.

Staying close to camp, we enjoyed the playful antics of the arctic hare bunnies. Rain didn't bother them. In their soft, fuzzy brown coats, they blended so well into the arctic tundra that when they sat very still we could scarcely see them. And if we couldn't see them, neither could a fox, a wolf or a snowy owl, their chief predators. But their parents were not nearly so lucky. We had no trouble spotting their startlingly white coats, even in the far distance. Here on Ellesmere, adult arctic hares don't turn brown in summer and we guessed it must be because the season is too short. They don't have time to turn brown and then white again before the first snows of autumn. But they do molt heavily, losing most of their last-winter coats as new hair grows in, and this gives them a rather scruffy, raggedy look as they lope across the tundra. One hare had lost so much fur from its bony face that it looked almost like a dog.

Our most exciting visitors came very early one morning. A long, lingering howl awakened us at six o'clock. I poked my head out the door of the tent and saw two white arctic wolves, rimmed in sunlight, standing on the high ridge above camp. As I watched, one of them howled again, a wild, haunting call that floated and echoed down the valley.

Never in our lives have we dressed so fast. Anyone watching from outside the tent might have thought there was a war going on inside as we thrashed about trying to find shirts and jeans, and socks that always managed to bury themselves in the bottoms of the sleeping bags. Tumbling out of the tent in record time, we grabbed our cameras and tripods and raced for the ridge.

One of the wolves had already disappeared, but the other — the larger — was still there. As I ran, tripping and stumbling over the tussocky tundra, with the heavy metal tripod digging sharply into my shoulder, the wolf lay down with its head between its feet, like a big dog, and watched me coming.

By the halfway mark my heart was pounding against my ribs and I was panting hard. I stopped, struggling to catch my breath, then began to walk forward, very slowly. I could see the wolf gazing at me with big, glowing amber eyes as I steadily closed the distance.

Closer... and closer.... Now the big wolf suddenly stood up. I stopped, eased the tripod off my bruised shoulder and watched, spellbound. Lifting its head, the wolf howled once more. Without pausing to think and in the excitement of the moment completely forgetting about my camera, I howled back. And then the wolf answered me!

It was a moment of pure magic. My voice is much higher pitched than a wolf's, more like the sound of a coyote. I have had some good moments conversing with those sociable animals back home on our farm and I wondered what this arctic wolf thought, hearing the call of his southern cousin. But I wasn't to know. The wolf wheeled around sharply and disappeared over the ridge top in a blur of smoky white.

"Did you get a picture?" John called out. I shook my head. In that moment, the sheer joy of being answered by an arctic wolf was worth far more than a picture.

We followed the wolves up the valley but with their long legs and easy stride, they soon outdistanced us, and vanished into the far hills.

The wolves came to our campsite every morning and every evening after that to howl. Perhaps they were curious about us, or just being sociable. Their strangely haunting calls filled my imagination. We tried again and again to get close to them but they always kept their distance and we never managed to get any really close-up photographs. But how lucky we were, to be sharing Tanquary Fiord with such wild and splendid creatures.

We camped at Tanquary for two weeks, hiking out across the tundra each day, and exploring the far valleys. Under a sun that never set, the days seemed to go on forever, and we fell into a wonderful pattern of sleeping only when we were tired and eating only when we got hungry. Time just didn't seem to mean anything out here, and I gladly stopped wearing my watch.

One afternoon a noisy helicopter descended into camp, bearing a small group of researchers and shattering our accustomed silence. Leaving the party to survey and hike around, we borrowed their helicopter for a few hours and persuaded the pilot to fly us into a neighboring valley. From the air, we soon spotted a little group of caribou, no more than four or five adults with a few small calves.

We landed well behind a low hill, then crept up, hoping to catch sight of them. Imagine our surprise when we rounded the top to find the caribou coming toward us, curious to see what we were. They were a little band of Peary caribou, named after the famous American explorer Robert Peary, who led an expedition to the North Pole in 1909. How small they were. I remembered the woodland caribou we had seen in Labrador with their huge racks of velvety antlers. These Peary caribou were tiny by comparison.

The caribou pawed the ground and sniffed the air, trying to get our scent. They have had few encounters with humans and, like most creatures in the High Arctic, they showed more curiosity than fear. Unfortunately, in the whole of the Arctic, there are not very many Peary caribou. Only a few thousand have been counted, and here on north Ellesmere no more than 13 have ever been seen at any one time. What a contrast to the mighty herds of barren-ground caribou that roam the vast territories to the south and west. There, a single herd can number more than 130,000.

We were counting down the days now. It was almost the middle of August and our long journey was coming to an end. Summer was also drawing to a close. The sun had begun to dip much lower behind the hills each night and there was more chill in the air.

And then one afternoon the Twin Otter arrived and it was time to go. We broke camp slowly, packing up all our belongings, rolling up the sleeping bags and folding the tent for the last time. How I would miss Tanquary Fiord...the arctic hare...the young bunnies...and especially the white wolves. I would soon have to start wearing a watch again and deal with the shorter days and dark nights back home. What a dismal thought! As we boarded the aircraft I took one last look out over the blue water of the fiord and up the long green valley, trying to burn the image of that arctic wilderness so deeply into my memory that it would last forever.

Too soon, we were airborne. But before setting a course south for Resolute, Duncan turned north and took us on one last breathtaking flight around the top of Ellesmere. We soared like a bird through Yalverton Pass, the Twin Otter dwarfed by its enormous glaciers, then up and over the jagged coastal mountains whose craggy peaks are wreathed in snowfields and crested with ice caps. Some of these mountaintops have never been seen, for they lie buried under 2,000 metres (6,500 feet) of snow and ice. Here, the mountains are still emerging from the Ice Age and some of that ice could be 100,000 years old.

Breaking out of the mountains, our small craft flew low along the northern coastline. Ahead of us was Ward Hunt Island, surrounded by its apron of ice, which never melts. And beyond it was the dark outline of Cape Columbia, the rocky tip of North America.

Beneath us the glittering frozen sea was fractured into a million tumbled ridges and I shielded my eyes against their dazzling brilliance, suddenly remembering how we had searched for harp seals in that same blinding brightness at the start of our journey. How long ago it seemed. I was filled with a wonderful sense of elation. We had begun our journey in Newfoundland and now here we were, flying right off the top of the map! Behind us lay the whole North American continent, stretching away beyond the curve of the horizon. Ahead, there was nothing but the North Pole. I grinned at John, and gave him a triumphant thumbs-up. Our journey to the top of the world was finally complete.

The Twin Otter turned in a slow, graceful arc over the sea. Sunlight sparkled on the metal wingtips as Duncan headed us back toward the land, and toward home.

Index